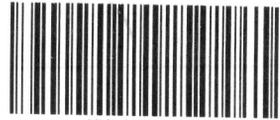

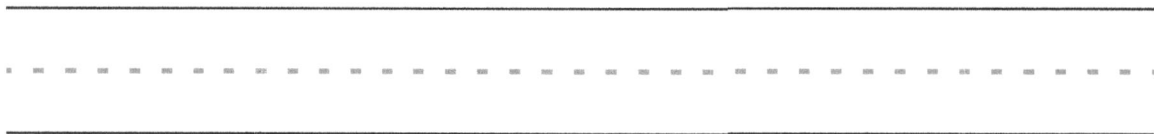

Made in the USA
Monee, IL
30 April 2022

95651808R00063